Poems From Earth

(A Flourishing Odyssey)

Wilhelm Höjer

For Sally Höjer!

"God did not invent death, and when living creatures die, it gives him no pleasure. He created everything so that it might continue to exist, and everything he created is wholesome and good. There is no deadly poison in them. No, death does not rule this world, for God's justice does not die. Ungodly people have brought death on themselves by the things they have said and done. They yearn for death as if it were a lover."

Book of Wisdom 1: 12-16

To the Reader

What is poetry but a reminder of how special our reality truly is. Poetry is a childlike reflection upon reality, playing with our words, capturing life in description. Poetry is a reminder of what we've often forgotten as adults, where we tend to live more in their minds than in our bodies, especially as we grow older. Yet children are always in their bodies, refusing to lose their carnality. Likewise, poetry refuses to let words lose their carnality. In poetry every word has flesh and breath, sound and inflection. This book of poems is a Mediterranean Odyssey which aspires to capture the life and carnality of a visit to *La Bella Italia*. It's an odyssey between the Scylla of Freedom and the Charybdis of Destiny. That is the reason for this collection. It is the author's hope that it will lead more people to discover themselves along its shores; this year, next year, or another year altogether, wherever we may stand on the horizon line.

Wilhelm Höjer

Kansas City, Missouri, September 14th, 2022

Contents

I

"Origins"

Here you were washed ashore
among the numerous starfish of Heaven
under your feet.

Here you began your pilgrimage
upon foreign land like a lizard which scurries
in a Roman ruin.

Here you found your family's poems
inside ancient marble crushed asunder by gravity
within an hourglass.

Here you saw your dreams fly
like a flock of wild birds before the morning light
over a cathedral.

Here you received the gift of words
as one tosses a fresh meat bone to a hungry dog
on a Persian rug.

Here you were introduced to pain
as the animalistic love between two yearning souls
in separate cages.

Here you still stand and stare
with the remembrance of all things directed inward
towards yourself.

II

"Arcady"

Someone touched you in Arcady,
somewhere in the fold...
Could someone spot you,
before you could see?

Light received you in a field, so quick and so bold.
If they abandoned you,
it was day in Arcady...
Life came to turn a key, in that vine-clad wold.

Uncertainty brought you unsung treasures to be...
Someone breathes softly on your skin's summer gold.
It might have been you,
my god of Arcady...!

III

"Sorrento"

An aroma of salt among rocks in the sea,
which forget time and when tides cease.
An old cathedral rests herself gently
against the towns afternoon peace.

A local people hurry slowly, come and leave,
over streets cracked with weeds and grass.
A life begins to see and can perceive
an ancient inheritance as they pass.

A young boy stands there silent and tall,
listens to the flow of his blood stream.
A high sea resounds where the small
but brave, strong life begins to dream.

An average wine glass stands on a table,
in the town's shifting light and shade.
A grapes nectar, poured for hands to cradle,
in a globe of glass, as a heavenly aid.

IV

"Amalfi"

Never certain, but always guessing
that free will inside your blood.
Always this hiss from the sea
without ever remembering
the first blue wave of the flood.

Maybe a belief, but never certain,
where you'll be beached the final night.
Yes, you passed muster one morning,
but only you know the course
from a chart mapped with your sight.

This anchor around your foot,
that burden of nothing at all,
is an easy inspiration to sail away
from every port, but lacking elders
into a circle that does not enthrall.

The pull of longing upon your back
is that eternal wind unknown.
It's the gust of escape in the sail
on a flowing, billowing sea of salt
from a source where tears have flown.

As a star in the sky on God's heaven
you sail beneath a rocky highland.
But in that ocean gap of uncertainty,
before drowning yourself in longing,
you've already become another's island.

V

"Capri"

It's true that life writes poetry -
isn't the dream also true?
We know that heavens mercy
seeks us all, not just a few.

Even if we set sail on a barren sea,
it's true that life writes poetry.
More real than our hands are two,
are often dreamlands in a golden hue.

More than all we can know and once knew,
more than even my home and country,
it's true that life writes poetry -
when wisdom sings, the world is anew.

Maybe on dry land with our crew,
after winds which summoned the sea,
we'll nods our heads in the morning dew -
it's true that life writes poetry.

VI

"Archimedes point"

In Siracuse stood a temple in life's busy chase,
consecrated to Athena, over the market-place.
It received Minerva's sign in that ancient town,
in order to serve the bay-leafed imperial crown.

The Romans were waiting by her marble side
when Saints Peter and Paul spoke to their pride,
when the apostles were so daring and overbold
as to gather the lost Sicilian sheep into a fold.

All then became of what Archimedes had seen
and learned of this world's blue and green,
a very holy church where we are humbly led
among stately pillars as we stumble and tread.

Where pillars themselves can wander in the light,
so still as they stand through both day and night
and become for the rest of us in this foreign land,
like an old friend, a good Shepherd for a lamb.

VII

"La Lingua Franca"

Maybe it's the song from a French chapelle,
but just as likely it is the presence of you
who rises in incense and rings in the bell,
who reunites my heart with a Christian clue.

A seven story mountain I have come to climb
and it's paths are steep, with bends and crooks.
It's written somewhere in the old dusty books
that eternity is reached in time...

My father is with me, through high and low,
even without being there to call me son,
almost without seeing him, I can surely know
that Gods creative work is always done.

The censor swings as life itself, I watch it allure
and bind our prayers to the sway of life and death.
I'll sing our hymn until my lungs hold no breath,
that my father lives, through his morte and amour.

VIII

"Rafaello: Girl with unicorn"

A wind which cools
your face in the portico hall.
A mist which sets
behind you at autumns fall.

A silhouette of your hair,
braided gold-brown and fair.
In your arms one of your kin,
a unicorn pure from sin.

Raphael painted you true,
has one picture room for two?

IX

"Italian Compass"

The ship of fools sails far away,
in tow our human moan.
Compass set for the philosopher stone
on a beach of senseless clay.

The captain reads under Diogenes lamp
of mans futile joy and pain.
He lifts his head, an ivory brain
and like his cabin - dark and damp.

May deep Atlantis rise,
from its mythic depths,
to make this pilot wise!

X

"Palermo"

Awoken here, by the helping hand
of a bird-song's be-winged creed.
The earth itself is like a waking reed -
the lapping waves and the shifting sand.

Awoken by a dream from the changing sea
...was I truly sailing there, in the rising sun,
out in a cool current, but what had I done
to deserve those trade-winds of immortality?

No, I was only there, where I am always near
that old perspective where I can look upon it,
that ancient instrument for a humble sonnet,
the beat of my own heart is playing there...

Birds they fly, while we remain, only to rise
bound to this earth, Newtons law is strong!
Listen carefully to the gravity of their song
and then find if insight can make us wise:

To know, to wake, to be and always behold,
to see that life is good and a splendid thing.
See the joyous crowds in summer or spring
embrace in love by burning bushes of gold.

See through twelve months and seven days
all the possibilities of these divided lands.

Grasp between your own two cupped hands
the dust diviner words than yours could raise.

Suddenly we believe in a day after tomorrow,
or is it all human relief and a fantasy in vain?
People are now awake, it all starts up again,
imagine all we can answer human sorrow...

 I thank you and this early hour,
in Gods light - blessings flower!

XI

"Fratelli d'Italia"

Life is contained in a blade of grass,
it shifts in the wind of father and son.
Storms came and will come to pass.

Judgement threatens us as we run
from all that has created our sorrow,
within both our women and our men.

All our days we lend and we borrow,
the torch has been handed us again
and made our eyes not quite tearless.

You must seek to know day after day
that brotherly love is always fearless -
I am still your truest friend, men say.

XII

"Urbis et Orbis"

When Rome calls - we go, every single number!
All the victorious and all the defeated,
all the waking and all those in slumber,
all of the feared and all of the entreated.

We lift our necks to see that only vestal fire,
burning ever since the first Roman breed
acquired the world in their temporal desire
and planted in free men a universal seed.

Still, mysteries were left across the Aegean,
in voices picking grapes from a Greek vine,
in talk around a table set for the new religion,
of life and death, only one Love could entwine.

XIII

"Solitude in Ravello"

Hear how it rains in this dreary town,
cascading tears from the giver of life.
Under the clouds, wet, dripping down,
He is weeping over our toil and strife.

So this silver night lies there sunken,
as fallen nature makes mud of dust
and the gutter looks sad and drunken,
reflecting heavens stars in wanton lust.

Hear how softly our sobbing mother
on the streets of love begins to sing
of a holy, bloody sacrifice for another,
a tempest from the sweat of our king.

Why sit down and write in this house,
hearing the Devils two black feet despair,
moving nimble past termite and louse,
breathing down my neck, raising my hair.

Hear how November rain begins to play
in the dingy drain, making the water spin.
See the soil and twigs, brown dirt and clay
form rich mandalas for all that enter in.

Maybe one day when the rain and wind
will carry away even my fleshy skeleton

we'll receive the last sign behind a blind,
as I leave to start my life already begun.

Remember, always, if you have fear,
I keep you close to my beating breast.
When I go, look around, use your ear,
I'm calling behind that crimson crest.

The day I am summoned to depart,
when puzzling drizzles of wind will whirl
and anxious eyes begin to fly and dart,
remember we shall never die, sweet girl...

If only you give me your hand,
we'll reach our promised land.

XIV

"First rays in Positano"

The new brighter day sees
more than birds and bees,
more than light and shade.

The new day contains all
our tales of rise and fall,
all love taken and made.

The night gives us all rest
for our worst and our best,
with dreams for boy and girl.

The night is also our hope,
helping man's mind to cope
under a moon's white pearl.

Life is God's creation risen,
a true gift, one freely given.
It is good, it is very good.

When true death arrives
before her animate eyes,
we sleep in a dark wood.

Has your courage wained?
Even more has been gained -
now all can be imagined too!

If the greatest gift has come
see that it has become
the day and night and you!

XV

"Two of us in Naples"

The two who recognized their treasure,
found that true love is the only measure
of their shared voices in a simple song,
side by side at a piano, soft and strong.

They wander on roads which have fled
from fakery, merging a heart and head.
God doesn't choose where they roam,
but still He knows that He is their home.

XVI

"Smiles under Vesuvius"

How beautifully you tread on the urban street
with worldly destruction in your mind's eye.
This concrete earth is filled with meet and greet
that dare not speak of things beyond the sky.

This city of light contains all the just words,
every just sentiment uttered from your throat,
giving flight to angels coming heavenwards,
who soar where church bells chime a note.

The reason you decided to even listen today
is why a windy breeze comes to clear the mist,
why the beauty of day can be both blue or grey,
why music was invented when lovers kissed.

The gilded towers ring out heavens laughter,
and I see your face change, every once in a while,
when the bells chime. I know one second after
that you have wings, in the moment you smile!

XVII

"Rome"

Everything is not Rome,
but Rome is everything.
Weathering a seasoned dome
is a spirit of fall and spring.

All that she can release,
win from passing time,
is the greatest peace,
her penance for our crime.

Rome, she reflects it
before we can see it.
All which is of grace
is her life's true face.

Sun and rain, passing gloom,
by spires and baroque bows,
falling where all shall bloom,
on ash, where we once rose.

XVIII

"Question and Answer with Thomas Aquinas"

We ask, what is that joy on our face
when the sun has dried up the rain,
when the day recently gave a trace
of a constant light that comes again?

We ask, how many bitter goodbyes
and hard lessons one life can hold?
How many tears and petulant cries
can cross the light - we are never told.

Everyone asks: what became of life,
what have I done, before all is too late
to enjoy day and sun, to heal from strife;
Or is it vain? Has death no pearly gate?

But does anybody ask, what do we do
when friendships are for our sake,
that is given to us all before we too
become lights for hearts that break?

XIX

"A friend on the piazza"

When you have a friend in town
every morning is a joy to share.
What magic lies beyond the stair!
Shadows are light, feathery down.

The sun shines for every reason,
when you have a friend in town.
You smile under tears as a clown,
curiously wise, in every season.

The meager day is a feast instead,
turning a sad frown upside down,
when you have a friend in town
to share the breaking of the bread.

The universe is one golden crown,
spotless and brightly gleaming,
worn by the world, daydreaming,
when you have a friend in town.

XX

"Coffee bar on the piazza"

On this square the coffee-tables do not look well:
Picasso-bodies, displaced, contorted wood-toys
built formless, but fixed, inside a neighborly hell,
where a silence of existence never bothers noise.

The empty steaming cups from new kitchen crypts,
amuse this new dead theater of persistent rumor.
Mouths sip, swallow and smirk as from old scripts
- the plague of laughter without a sense of humor.

If an eastern wind would blow over this slow sod,
maybe a buried thought could then be resurrected
and empty cups be filled with The Word; one nod,
one fiat would heal us - we would stand corrected.

While we stumble along to touch something stable,
searching for some foreign reality in a distant land,
already on mother earth we can sit by a solid table,
always with a blood filled cup held in Adam's hand.

XXI

"Navigating a friendship: Per sempre"

We can know a friendship forever more,
an undulating feeling so deep and clear,
as when sails are cast over sea and oar
to greet the wide world without any fear.

Yes, if we only serve what is always true
we can know a friendship forever more.
Greater in glory and power are the few,
the happy few, who navigate to this shore.

If we see the pure strength of the flower
growing as the tree from the same core,
we can know a friendship forever more,
as blossoming petals in a garden bower.

To the sun even humble weeds will soar
and by labor rise up through dirt and clay.
Watch them and learn that already today
we can know a friendship forever more.

XXII

"Advent"

I light a candle with a flame
and reflect on my travelings:
I know that Heaven's name
hides behind created things.

To cast these things aside
to touch life's forbidden land,
is actually to have denied
that grace is a hidden hand.

If shadows form a pattern
of life and death by the light,
I see, seated in my cavern,
that all is for God's delight.

I see the one fountain of life,
more than our joy and fear,
more than the pen and knife,
is love itself, love ever near.

So speaks all we have heard,
said, seen and have done -
reflected in that creative word
when God spoke in his son.

XXIII

"Poet on Ischia"

All the songs that are yours
I hear as stars begin to shine.
Closing my eyes, opening doors,
they sound as if they were mine.

All the days which are ours
through the years and the times,
gives me joy as my knee cowers,
enhancing these difficult climbs.

All of life's words and delights
shared with you as wine and bread,
has this small death we call night,
sing to my heart's rhythmic thread.

XXIV

"Pensive wine in Tuscany"

Dante's vineyard can enchant,
we are his children, in a row,
and all we can harvest and plant
again, if we water and we sow.

It never ends, we live on land
by gifts which the earth fulfills.
The comedy is that we demand
and bind, not freeing up our wills.

Here, between the wine and briar,
with light and air around my skin,
I become so gleeful in the mire,
like these grapes for God and kin...

I declare: what rhymes with Chianti
but some words between you and me,
in Tuscan districts we so inflagranti
 are admonished to become santi?

Always something true and holy
is found in those voices from tanti!
We must continue on and avanti,
smile and drink more of this Chianti...

XXV

"The lunatic light - Solitude"

The moon, it hangs low in the distance
but is close to us with its present light.
Through the night flows a sustenance,
a harvest moon warms us in our plight.

In it's aura, as clean and clear as it sits,
it is the night's very partaking in the sun.
It is hard to hear it from popular pulpits
that this is life's answer arisen and come.

If you ask, very hopelessly and distraught,
why anxiety has made your evening weary,
know that for light and hope to be caught,
the darkness seems completely necessary.

XXVI

"La bella donna con la gitarra"

Yes, so wonderful it is to see you
united with your brown guitar.
In your notes I hear myself too
and know your song is not bizarre.

You compose as you always live,
you sing just as you are to me:
a breeze which decides to give
from our spirits own vocabulary.

So still and sweet I hear the song
made of embers - which is strength.
The new sunrise for which we long
stretch along your horizons length.

It is your soul which sings aloud,
and such a heart will never cease
to touch the ears that wrap a shroud
of living love around your peace.

The gentle hope which leads you on
to travel with purpose a melodic path,
atones for any soul you never won,
your smile is my truth: existential math.

Forever shall your own female voice
give life to the message from up high,
that your lips sing of a good choice
to include all in a God for you and I.

XXVII

"Verona"

Time does not stay,
time is meant to cleave.
Give me a sign today,
speak before you leave.

Don't break every bond,
don't prolong the pain.
You must try to respond,
give me your hand again.

Go then, my best friend,
go to your new love, flee.
Take the letter I penned,
give my heart back to me.

XXVIII

"Asleep on Via Appia"

Is God asleep when the ancient bird
sways and swings where summer's kept;
when the words you forgot you heard,
arrive at the ruins where you slept?

Is it true that heaven is asleep
when the little pilot skylarks
fly with the goldcrests in steep
paths over lakes and wild parks?

Is God asleep in the whirl of stars
who greet the earth and one another?
Is heaven away between Venus and Mars
when a girl becomes a new mother?

Is God asleep when an old grand-pa
with his children and grandchildren
set out as summer begins to withdraw
and cold attacks our women and men?

Is it true that heaven is asleep
when a dream becomes reality;
when suddenly he hears her weep:
"You and me for eternity!"

Is God asleep when Grieg and Verdi
write their summer concert?
Is heaven sleeping still and sturdy
when poets form life from dirt?

XXIX

"Sorrento in September"

This is how you should live and see,
this is how you should listen and yearn,
among the lemon trees growing for you!

No one has any greater joy or glee,
when dreams are sealed in a Grecian urn,
than the man who lives now to pursue!

Always within the next pondering
that comes willfully slow or driven,
you see inside that inverted glow

of God's gaze above your wandering,
of every gift which the dream has given,
that it was you who was born to know.

XXX

"The Latin Nation"

We are a nation onto ourselves,
who are the slaves of the Latins.
A beloved alphabet on our shelves,
as sacred as Vespers and Matins.
And the heart has reasons minds know not,
for loving declensions Virgil wrought.
This language has blessed the thought
of men dressed in rags to silks and satins.

Our spiritual home is the Pantheon,
by emperors, martyrs and countless others.
The national insignia that we put on,
carries the red Pompeiian colors.
Faunus has given us his ancient fife,
to praise Carmenta, our lettered wife,
in our divinely graced but earthly life,
as new generations become our brothers.

We are a little band at the feet of sages,
a small affinity in the cultural sector.
A line is drawn by Cato to Christian ages,
according to every lector and Nestor.
They salute with *Ave*! and give correction,
for our nation needs their direction,
ennobling us despite our imperfection -
they are as formidable as Hector!

Soon it shall be three thousand years
of the *Ab Urbe Condita* traditions.
Suddenly a grand old vision appears
of consuls, caesars, plebs and patricians,
Roman numerals and vocabulary,
brick and marble, the classical library,
the republic's rise and fall in January,
Mediterranean wars and ambitions.

But soon again Latin will be quoted,
in every youth who reads his Cicero
or Dante, who's echo from our Ovid
will reestablish the Roman *status quo*.
Yes, once again shall our bacchanal
be in Cathedrals and the diaconal
ministers sing as Solomons canticle,
to a loving cup filled to overflow!

Yes, we shall defend the Roman law,
and we will win the laurel crown.
So stand before our myth in awe,
where in a cave, by a she-wolf, we lie down,
and then rise to proclaim our creed:
that to *Urbi et Orbi* all must concede!
But if our flowers grow with weeds,
it's to convert the world through one town.

Soon we shall rule over people and lands
by giving our daily offerings,
with reverence and humble hands
in praise for what the choir sings,
from Gregorian chant to Palestrina:

about Jesus and Mary, our Rex and Regina,
as doves and lilies in a bloody arena -
that is what our nationality brings.

Across the seven hills is St.Peter's basilica
built by prayers where bells are rung:
it's the holiest sanctuary on this peninsula -
in the body of Christ it's our spiritual lung.
It breathes its breath over the Vestal fire
burning on embers which never tire.
The deepest truth it confronts to every liar,
is that the devil hates the Latin tongue!

XXXI

"A motor-bird over Italy"

As a ship in the sky, a metallic bird
is seen in the air, engines heard.

Somebody cries: "what a terrible roar,
over the land doves should soar!"

Yes where angels fly, she makes a stir -
it's hard to admit which flight I prefer…

For is it not better to pray,
over the clouds above,
for better views of sanity?

And is it more valid to say,
both we and the peaceful dove,
together share laws of gravity?

XXXII

"The Fly"

A fly has slowly risen
from sleep after evening Mass.
Searching my table with a mission
- a nose dive into the wine glass.

The fly cannot know what know treasure
lies buried in sunken pleasure.
For death cannot play strong for long
facing a baptism of eternal song.

The fly bids goodbye to what has fled
without a reflection on being dead.
A being stands at a crossroads again,
soon it will have no strength but pain.

But we can answer when we meet,
that we can reflect deeper on our seat,
- if only to listen to the word
that no fly can hear, nor any bird.

If you see the fly quiver in it,
drunk in a last lazy minute,
then let exit from your throat
a more meaningful note.

This is how we should live and play,
for death will soon be here today,

so think, and don't simply strive,
only because you are alive.

For thought is for another's smile,
the one's we meet here for awhile.
Then we can wander with laughter
and rise to heaven's blue thereafter.

The fly rises when evening is late,
yet crawls away to a given fate.
Death for all will come, to enter in
with the life we soon shall begin.

XXXIII

"The Doorway"

How quickly the doors of perception change,
but quietly,
without thunder and lightning,
almost unnoticeably.
Yet what has changed?
When life is still life,
the sun the same sun,
the clouds the same clouds.
When possessions are not more than that,
when friends are friends,
when the joy of seeing and hearing, giving and receiving,
is the same.
Then nothing has changed,
nothing has been lost or found.

All is of a greater will.
All is a gift.
All is to be
in this world
for as long as it lasts.

So what has changed so quickly?
Everything and nothing.
We are all the same -
created to share the light,
created to die -
another day.

XXXIV

"The Sea"

The sea
flows to my eye
and flows out
where you are seen
by the sky
which sees the sea.

The sea
flows to my eye
and flows out
where you are seen
by the sky
which sees the sea.

The sea
flows to my eye
and flows out
where you are seen
by the sky
which sees the sea.

XXXV

"The Mediterranean Light"

When the sun goes down in the west,
we look towards evening lands.
When the sun rises in the east,
I see God's own silver sands.

When the light sinks in you,
it darkens my own mind too.
When the sun warms your cheek,
it shines as bright in me.

When words are spoken between us,
I believe that life is still true,
I know that yet another day, must
hold a pearl in the shell of a clue.

When the night says goodbye
to the day with a wave and a cry,
on the horizon I see your next smile
approaching for many a-mile.

When everything has turned stupidly sad,
it turns again to good from bad;
then I can hear, as the last time,
a song of poetry and rhyme.

When crumbs can become a feast,
I always remember: love is a choice.
The Light, The Strong One from the east,
comes to me through your voice.

XXXVI

"The White Rose"

The sun, it shines upon my face.
My thoughts run in circles,
about everything and nothing, in and out of space,
the false and the true - all those hurdles.

As a glimpse of two seconds on a snow-white day,
as knowledge in my memories rest,
eternity can shed light on what has fled away,
on all the moments of life
you breathed with your chest.

And it glitters in those drops that have fled
my glass dripping south.
I can always look up what I read
and not have to open my mouth.

Then one day which will be the last,
but then also the first,
not one soul shall longer thirst,
but learn what we knew from our past:

That all life is a gift, as the oriented sky
is as generous as it is unique to my eye.
All that which is mine, I'll tell you true,
is part of the inheritance - that's life too,
even after I die.

So, what demands shall be right to crave of life? Tell me
as words come to pass.
"Thank you," says more than all life can tell.

XXXVII

"Canto 33"

The light in the night
from a distant shore,
the life that's in sight
is a lifetime more.

Our minutes are given.
But beyond this gift,
which gives as leaven,
and so rises to lift,

is always something more,
something so true,
something we see and implore,
something found in a clue.

To seek life and to see,
almost nothing of everything.
To live, cry, smile and be,
to know we fell from something.

But know nonetheless,
all you do, all you are,
resembles yourself. Yes,
as the sun is a star.

Perhaps only now,
you see what you know,

past the why and the how,
it is love, watch it grow!

Light enhances everything.
Darkness made life and man.
When we truly learn to sing,
we'll see how it all began.

Now hear it be said,
know it happens for sure,
when each night is fed
with life, it lives more.

Sing, my good friend,
the night does you good,
sing and then sing again,
to be better understood.

I listen when you croon,
the night sings in tune,
as if it were you,
yes, as if it were you!

XXXVIII

"Garda Lake"

A growing moon shines
high over Garda Lake.
It nods to lights that embrace
the lake where people live.

I sit with wine and stare
out over Garda Lake.
I see how glimmers dance
on the water where life grows.

The warmth of the darkness,
lightly around Garda Lake,
contains nature's forms
which recognize their mother.

A source never freezing into ice
is this Garda Lake.
A stream of life never ending,
spreading its eternal light.

It's not a analysis
which describes Garda Lake,
but you and I who think
that the power of grace is great.

If the clouds should ever cover
and close over Garda Lake,

the lake is as armor
against a teared up earth.

I answer with the moon,
as it recedes from Garda Lake,
that rhymes do not prevail,
and no one shall never die.

I answer with the moon's own words:
"thank's for the light,"
from a brother.

XXXIX

"Trenitalia"

A train on new tracks, always on old roads.
Just to know that gives me more than I own,
traveling through the green.

I notice how white sheep never seem to understand
the hour's path into years under a rain
heavy sky.

A town is born to life, is it yours or mine, who knows?
Life is wherever we live, as the the train goes
further north.

I'm not so far from you, and not to forget,
the journey takes the path of love, soon we
both will be home.

The trees pass by my window
stretched out along the river bank.
Men and women make scenes
as if nothing before had happened.
The bridges which takes us over
this stretch of life's waters,
carries with them all that sleeps
underway towards new lands.

Wine still grows on the ground
and the train it sails in wine.

Always on board the arc -
us! And my covenant is yours.
A seed flies inside the wind
swiftly towards Heaven and sea.
It touches, slightly, our earth,
is silhouetted by the night,
so grateful for all that came.

But even all that never came,
is a sign of love from your God!

XL

"Halo's in the night"

There walks a man on the streets,
his town is the world's town.
Where others talk, he greets
his joy and pain with silence.

But those who can hear and see,
knows all he goes around and thinks.
Through streets that don't agree
with all that others forget.

If somebody, sometime, saw him,
as he walks there now,
then the world would receive him
as the gift they did not see.

Who is this man, my friend?
Who's wisdom lifts him high over land
where all his heartaches end -
that were not meant for him…

Insights into his art
is a book he threw away:
wisdom is a sorrow of the heart.
Beautiful is the man who knows that

no other pain is greater than love.
He teaches what I think I know:

how light shines on in Heaven above,
how night begets a new day.

An old woman sits alone,
recalls a time when she was young…
A little black bench is her throne,
she knows that life exists.

Even if her old age is hard,
she sees a little girl and a boy…
All are the same: though scarred,
we'll be ourselves before the end.

If somebody, sometime, saw them,
as they appear there now,
then the world would receive them
as the gifts they did not see.

XLI

"Genua - Castle in the Sand"

My castle in the sand stands strong
against weather and wind,
It stands delicate in my mind -
for it is built upon faith.

It stands built with longing,
built by children's hands.
My sand castle is a dream,
it can't fall by the water's tide.

I live inside this castle,
with a thousand lost words.
They fill the town, sea and beach
with faith in what is true.

There is room for all I see,
giving me more and more.
I own hall after hall, I own
space for all I want to say.

One day, I will take us here.
Here, where the sun goes down.
Here, by the distant sea. Here
where Columbus made his wish.

Here, where he did not understand
where in the world he went.

Here, where we later knew
that all we can see is eternity.

Here, where we look west,
to a better dream than the rest.
Here, where we see that our world
happens by God's holy word.